I DIDN'T DESERVE YOU

Love can be blinding. Rage can be deadly.

But revenge? Revenge is patient.

Written By
AUGUST CLAY

For more information, or to book an event, contact:

Augustclaystories@gmail.com or visit www.augustclaystories.com

Dedication

For the silenced voices who seek justice,

May their stories never be forgotten.

Acknowledgment

I want to extend my deepest gratitude to everyone who has joined me on this journey. To my readers, thank you for embracing the raw and heartbreaking story of Caleb and Isla. Your willingness to walk alongside these characters through their struggles means more than I can express.

To my family and friends, your unwavering support and encouragement have been my foundation. Thank you for standing by me through every chapter of this journey.

A special thanks to my editor, Orbit Book Writers, and the incredible team who helped bring this story to life. Your dedication and expertise have made all the difference.

Table Of Contents

Prologue

Caleb Whitfield wasn't always the man he had become. In the small town of Barrowsville, Texas, he was known as the dependable mechanic, the guy with grease-stained hands and an easy smile. People trusted him. When an engine stalled, or a tire went flat, Caleb was the one they called. Reliable and hardworking. A man who knew how to fix things.

But some things couldn't be fixed.

Behind closed doors, the cracks in Caleb's world ran deeper than anyone knew. His charm, the very thing that made him well-liked, masked something darker—a need for control that turned his love into something twisted. And Isla Hart, the woman who had once seen the best in him, was slowly realizing that love shouldn't feel like a cage.

Their relationship had started like any whirlwind romance—late-night drives down empty roads, whispered confessions under a sky full of stars, a passion that burned hot enough to feel like forever. Isla was ten years younger, full of life, an artist with wild dreams of opening her own studio. She carried a lightness in her spirit, the kind that made people lean in when she spoke, and made them believe that maybe the world was still beautiful.

But Caleb didn't want beautiful. He wanted obedience.

The storms in their relationship had begun as mere warning signs—a sharp word here, a disapproving glance there. She should call him when she got home. She should dress a little differently. She should tell him where she was going and who she was with. Small things, harmless things, or so she told herself.

Until the whispers turned into arguments, the arguments into slammed doors, and the slammed doors into bruised wrists and apologies spoken through clenched teeth.

Megan, Isla's best friend, noticed first—the way her laughter had dulled, how hesitation crept into her voice whenever Caleb's name came up, how the fire that once burned so brightly in her eyes had started to dim. But Isla wasn't ready to see the truth. Not yet.

Because he loved her, didn't he?

Love was supposed to be consuming. Love was supposed to hurt sometimes, wasn't it?

She held onto that hope for longer than she should have, convincing herself that the Caleb she fell for was still there, buried beneath his temper. That the man who once traced constellations on her skin in the dark hadn't been replaced by someone else.

But love wasn't supposed to make her afraid to breathe.

And the night she realized that was the night she knew she had to leave.

What Isla didn't know was that leaving would come at a price. That when Caleb felt something slipping from his grasp, he didn't just let go—he tightened his grip.

And some people never make it out of a grip like that.

Chapter One:
The Calm Before

The scent of oil and metal filled Caleb's workshop, mingling with the fading warmth of a late afternoon sun. Isla leaned against the doorway, her laughter blending with the low hum of a radio playing a country tune in the background. She watched Caleb as he tightened the last bolt on a customer's car, his hands steady and practiced, every movement precise.

When he glanced up and caught her eye, he gave her that easy smile that had once made her feel like the luckiest woman in Barrowsville.

"You look like you're a million miles away, sweetheart," he said, wiping his hands on a grease-stained rag.

"Penny for your thoughts?"

Isla's smile faltered for a moment, but she forced a lightness into her tone, brushing off the unease that had been lingering in the pit of her stomach.

"Just thinking about my art class tonight. Mrs. Harper's finally letting me use the studio for my own projects."

Caleb leaned back against the car, crossing his arms over his chest, a small crease forming between his brows.

"You're spending a lot of time at that studio, aren't you?" he said, his voice casual but carrying an edge she couldn't quite ignore. "Seems like you're hardly ever home these days."

Isla shifted on her feet, a knot tightening inside her. She tried to keep her voice steady.

"It's just… it's important to me, Caleb. You know that. I've been dreaming of this for years."

He studied her, his smile fading, gaze sharpening as if searching for something hidden beneath her words. After a moment, he pushed off the car and took a step closer, the air between them thickening with unspoken tension.

"Yeah, but it's starting to feel like it's more important than us, Isla," he said, his tone carrying a hint of accusation.

"You used to spend your evenings here with me. Now, it's like you can't wait to get out the door."

Isla forced a breath, reaching out to touch his arm, hoping the gesture might soften the edge in his voice. But her hand trembled slightly, betraying the uncertainty she tried to hide.

"It's not like that, Caleb," she said, trying to keep the plea out of her voice.

"I just... I need something that's mine, you know? My own little piece of the world."

Caleb's expression remained unreadable; the warmth that once drew her in was now replaced by something harder. He reached out, his hand wrapping around her wrist—not hard, but firm enough that she felt the unspoken warning beneath his touch.

Her pulse quickened.

"You don't need anything outside of this, Isla," he murmured, his voice tinged with something bitter.

"Outside of me. I'm all you need."

She pulled her hand back slowly, forcing herself to meet his gaze even though her legs felt like they might give out beneath her.

"That's not fair, Caleb," she whispered. "You don't get to decide what I need."

For a moment, the silence between them was thick enough to cut. His jaw tightened, and she saw a flicker of something dark in his eyes—something that sent a shiver racing down her spine.

Then, just as quickly, he exhaled sharply and stepped back. The tension in his shoulders eased, and he forced a smile, but it didn't reach his eyes.

"You're right. I'm sorry," he said, his tone lighter now, though a sharp edge still lingered beneath.

"Just... don't forget about me, okay? Don't forget that I'm the one who's always been here for you."

Isla nodded, returning his smile with one of her own, but it felt brittle in her chest. She slipped her hands into her coat pockets, turning toward the workshop door, the weight of his words pressing against her like a too-tight embrace.

As she walked out into the evening air, she couldn't shake the sense that something had shifted between them—something she didn't know how to put back in place.

Behind her, Caleb's voice followed, carrying a note of something colder that clung to her skin.

"Be home early tonight, Isla," he called, his smile dropping the moment her back was turned. "I'll be waiting."

She didn't look back as she made her way down the gravel path, her steps quickening with a quiet urgency she couldn't quite name. The air around her seemed to press in, the sky deepening with dusk, and the echo of his words lingered in her mind, making the shadows stretch longer than they should have.

As she walked away, she wrapped her arms around herself against the evening chill, but the unease settled deeper inside her, a whisper of dread she couldn't ignore.

She reached her car and slipped into the driver's seat, exhaling slowly. Her fingers trembled slightly as she pulled the seatbelt across her body, waiting for the soft click to ground her. The air inside was still, but it carried a familiar scent—faint traces of oil and paint, remnants of long drives, of nights spent chasing a dream that always seemed out of reach.

She exhaled, resting her forehead against the steering wheel, the weight of the past settling in her bones.

This car had been with her through it all. The miles of open road, the endless search for something more. It had broken down once, years ago, in a storm much like this creeping dusk. And Caleb had been the one to fix it.

That was the first time she had met him. Back then, she had thought she was lucky.

She had always been running, always searching for a place to belong. She had no memories of her homeland, only flashes of chaos—the sound of explosions and the cries of people she could no longer picture. War had stolen everything before she even understood what she had lost. Her parents. Her home. The only thing she had left was a memory of her mother's voice singing to her at night and the warmth of a hand guiding her through crowds of fleeing bodies. Then, the cold emptiness when that hand slipped away forever…

Leaving her a child with no home and no history.

At five years old, she had arrived in America alone, orphaned, barely speaking a word of English—a stranger in a foreign land where even her own name felt like something borrowed.

Barrowsville, Texas, became her new home—a fresh start, a second chance. The family that took her in, Megan's parents, gave her safety, love, and a chance at something better. But as she grew older, something inside her remained unsettled, like a puzzle piece that never quite fit.

At eighteen, she left, chasing independence, determined to stand on her own. Megan had pleaded with her to stay, but she wouldn't hear it. She was determined to carve her own path. She had to prove she could survive on her own, to build something for herself without the safety net of her adoptive family.

So, she became a traveling artist, chasing inspiration, sketching strangers on busy sidewalks, and painting murals in exchange for rent. Life was unpredictable, often unforgiving—but it was hers. She had told herself she was free and that she was doing exactly what she was meant to do.

Then came that night—the rain, the stalled engine. The mechanic who had appeared like some kind of savior, offering warmth and kindness when she needed it most: Caleb.

He had been kind, offering her his jacket while he worked. He had fixed her car without hesitation, refusing to take a cent for it. Instead, he handed her his number with an easy smile, telling her to call if she ever needed anything.

And she had.

She had called Caleb after that. She had let him in.

And now, years later, sitting in the same car he once saved, she wished she never had.

She straightened, adjusting the rearview mirror with steady hands. The unease still clung to her, wrapping around her ribs like a vice.

A shadow moved behind her in the reflection.

Her breath caught.

But when she twisted around, there was nothing.

Swallowing hard, she gripped the wheel and started the engine, forcing herself not to look back as she pulled onto the road.

Chapter Two:
Dark Clouds

Isla had always found solace in her art, a place where the world made sense in colors and strokes, where she could escape from the tension that seemed to wrap tighter around her life with each passing day. That evening, she stayed late at the studio, losing herself in the swirl of paint on canvas, the familiar rhythm of the brush against the easel.

Hours slipped by unnoticed until she realized the sun had long set, the streets outside dark and quiet.

By the time she arrived home, it was close to midnight. She parked her car in the driveway, the gravel crunching beneath her tires, and made her way up the front steps. The house was dark, save for a sliver of light spilling from the living room window.

She hesitated, sensing the unease that hung in the air, but steeled herself and turned the key in the lock.

As she pushed open the door, the smell of whiskey hit her like a wall. Caleb sat slouched in the worn leather chair near the window, a half-empty bottle clutched in one hand. His eyes flicked up to meet hers, and even in the dim light, she could see the glint of accusation that lurked in their depths.

"You're late," he muttered, his voice slurring slightly, though there was nothing sluggish about the sharp edge beneath his words. "Real late."

Isla dropped her keys on the small table by the door, trying to keep her movements steady even as her heart began to pound in her chest. She forced a smile, hoping to keep the conversation light, but it felt brittle on her lips.

"I lost track of time at the studio. You know how it is when I get into my work."

Caleb leaned forward, setting the bottle down with a heavy thud on the coffee table.

"Yeah, I know how it is," he said, his voice low, almost a growl. "But you sure you weren't meeting someone? Some guy, maybe?"

Her stomach twisted, a familiar dread creeping in. They had been down this road before, Caleb's jealousy rearing its head, transforming a harmless night out with friends or a late evening at the studio into something sinister in his mind.

She took a deep breath, trying to keep her tone even.

"Caleb, you've been drinking. You know that's not true."

He stood up suddenly, and the room seemed to shrink around them. He took a step closer, and she could see the tightness in his jaw, the flush creeping up his neck.

"Don't you dare try to turn this on me," he snapped, his voice rising. "You think I don't see the way you look when you're out? Like you're too good for this place, too good for me?"

She held up her hands, trying to calm him down.

"I'm not trying to turn anything on you, Caleb. But I'm not doing this tonight. I'll stay at Megan's place if I have to, but I'm not staying here with you like this."

The change was instant, like a mask slipping. His smile flattened, and the kindness that once made her heart flutter evaporated, replaced by a simmering fury that made the hair on the back of her neck stand on end.

He stepped closer, backing her against the wall, his frame towering over her, the muscles in his jaw tightening.

"What's that supposed to mean, Isla?" he hissed, his voice low and dangerous, the kind that made her stomach twist with dread.

She tried to hold her ground, but her voice wavered.

"I—Caleb, I can't stay here with you acting like this," she managed, pressing herself against the wall as if she could somehow disappear into the paint. "You're different when you drink, that's all."

He let out a bitter laugh, the sound cutting through the air like a blade. His hand shot out, slamming into the wall beside her head with a force that made the pictures rattle.

Isla flinched, her breath catching in her throat. The room seemed to blur for a moment. Heart pounding. Ears ringing. She barely had time to react before his fingers clamped around her wrist, squeezing hard—too hard.

Pain shot up her arm. She gasped. The walls felt like they were closing in, her vision narrowing to the dark fury in his eyes.

"You're not leaving me, Isla," he whispered, his breath hot against her skin.

"Not now, not ever. You're mine."

The slap came fast—a sharp, stinging blow that sent her stumbling sideways. A metallic taste filled her mouth. The floor tilted beneath her. She barely registered hitting the ground before he was on her again, his hands rough, unrelenting.

A boot connected with her ribs. A shockwave of pain rippled through her. She tried to curl in on herself, but another kick forced the breath from her lungs. A broken sound escaped her lips, something between a cry and a whimper.

"Caleb, please!" she choked out, her voice barely more than a desperate whisper, but he didn't hear her—or maybe he just didn't

14

care. The rage in his eyes had consumed him, turning him into a stranger she couldn't reason with, a monster that wouldn't relent.

It felt like forever. And then, suddenly, it was over.

Silence. Footsteps retreating. A door creaked shut.

She lay there, the cold floor pressing against her cheek. Her ears rang. Her body throbbed in places she didn't want to think about. She willed herself to move, but everything felt distant like she wasn't inside her own skin.

Minutes passed. Maybe hours.

She blinked. Breathed. The tears burned, but she let them fall this time.

That night, as she lay in the darkness, she made a promise to herself. She would not let this be her story. She would find a way out, even if it meant tearing apart the life they'd built together.

Chapter Three:
Bitter Winds

Isla awoke on the living room sofa, her head pounding and her body sore in places she didn't want to think about. She had fallen asleep on the floor, where she had landed after Caleb's rage had subsided. But now, she was tucked under a blanket, her body aching as she shifted slightly, trying to piece together the blurry events of the previous night.

The faint sound of Caleb singing drifted from the kitchen, an unsettlingly cheerful tune that clashed with the violence of the night before. Her heart hammered in her chest as she listened to his voice rise and fall, the sound of dishes clinking adding to the sense of unreality that washed over her. She closed her eyes for a moment, willing herself to stay calm.

The singing stopped, and she heard his footsteps approach, each one sending a jolt through her already frayed nerves. Caleb appeared in the doorway, a tight smile stretched across his face. He leaned down, brushing a kiss against her forehead. Isla flinched, the movement slight but enough to make his smile waver for a fraction of a second.

"Morning, sweetheart," he murmured, his voice too smooth, too normal. "I made you breakfast. Your favorite."

He set a plate of pancakes and a glass of apple juice on the coffee table, the smell turning her stomach. She stayed silent, staring at the food as he knelt beside the couch, his expression shifting to something softer, almost remorseful.

"I'm so sorry, Isla," he said, his voice breaking slightly. "I don't know what came over me last night. I... I was drunk, and I made a mistake. I swear it'll never happen again."

He reached for her hand, but she pulled back, curling her fingers into her lap. A flicker of something crossed his face—hurt, frustration, but it was gone as quickly as it came.

"I have to head to work now," he continued, his tone shifting back to that practiced gentleness. "Why don't you rest a bit longer? We'll talk about everything when I get home, okay?"

Without waiting for an answer, he pressed another quick kiss to her forehead, then grabbed his keys and left, the door clicking shut behind him.

As the sound of his car faded, Isla finally let out the breath she had been holding. She moved slowly, her body protesting with each step as she made her way to the bathroom. The moment she caught her reflection in the mirror, she froze.

A bruise marred her left cheek, deep purple spreading beneath her eye. Her lips were swollen, and a cut ran along the corner of her mouth. She stared at the face in the mirror, barely recognizing herself. The tears came then, silently streaming down her face as she leaned against the sink, her mind spinning with questions she couldn't yet answer.

She didn't hear the knock on the door at first, lost in her thoughts, but it grew more insistent. She wiped her face hastily and made her way to the front door. When she opened it, Megan stood on the other side, a bright smile on her face and a small gift bag in hand. Megan's smile faded as she took in Isla's appearance, her expression shifting to one of concern.

"Isla, what the—what happened to you?" Megan's voice was sharp, filled with worry as she stepped inside without waiting for an invitation. She reached out as if to touch Isla's bruised face, but Isla flinched back, her eyes darting to the door, her heart pounding as she imagined Caleb's reaction if he knew Megan was here.

"It's nothing," Isla muttered, turning away, her voice shaky. "I just—had a fall, that's all."

Megan's eyes narrowed, her disbelief evident. "Don't lie to me, Isla. I know you better than that." She caught Isla's arm, forcing her to meet her gaze. "This isn't just a fall. Tell me what happened. Was it Caleb?"

Isla hesitated, swallowing hard against the lump in her throat. She saw the determination in Megan's eyes, the way she refused to look away. And in that moment, the walls she had built around herself began to crack. She sank down onto the sofa, her shoulders slumping as the words tumbled out.

"It's been happening for a while now," she admitted, her voice barely above a whisper. "He... he has these moods, and when he drinks, it's like he's a different person. I tried to leave before, but he always... finds a way to make me stay."

Megan's face paled, her hands clenching into fists at her sides. "Isla, you can't stay here. He's dangerous. You need to go to the police. You need to file charges—"

"I can't," Isla's voice broke, her hands twisting together in her lap. "I'm scared of what he'll do if I leave. He'll... he'll come after me. He always does."

Megan knelt in front of her, gripping her hands tightly.

"Then let's get you out of here. You can come stay with me. We'll pack up your things and leave before he comes back. And when you're ready, we'll go to the police together. I'll be with you every step of the way."

Isla stared at her friend, seeing the fierce determination in her eyes, and for the first time in months, she allowed herself to feel a flicker of hope. She nodded slowly, the decision settling in her chest like a weight lifted.

"Okay. I'll pack my things."

They moved quickly, gathering Isla's belongings, but they didn't know that Caleb had logged into the home security system. From his phone, he watched the scene unfold, his expression darkening as he listened to their whispered conversation. Isla had no idea that her desperate attempt to escape would set in motion a night of terror that would change everything.

Chapter Four:
The Brooding Sky

C aleb returned home to an eerie silence. He already knew what he would find, but the emptiness of the house still hit him like a punch to the gut. His eyes swept over the living room, and a bitter laugh escaped his lips when he saw the untouched breakfast sitting on the coffee table, the pancakes now cold, the glass of apple juice still full.

He stalked toward the table, breathing heavily, and with a sudden roar, he flipped it over, sending the plate shattering against the wall, juice splattering across the floor. He grabbed a nearby chair and hurled it into the wall, watching it splinter with a sense of twisted satisfaction. The chaos spread—picture frames smashed, furniture upended, anything within reach met the full force of his fury.

But soon, the rage turned inward. He sank down onto the floor in the midst of the destruction, his chest heaving, tears beginning to spill. He pressed his fists against his temples as if trying to squeeze out the thoughts that tormented him.

"How could she do this to me?" he muttered through gritted teeth, his voice breaking. "After everything... after all I did for her. She's so ungrateful... so ungrateful."

Memories flashed through his mind—how he had found Isla when she was struggling. How he had helped her. How he made her feel special. In his twisted perception, he had been the one to lift her up, to care for her when no one else would. He had loved her, hadn't he? He had given her everything.

And this—this was how she repaid him?

His shoulders shook with sobs, his hands clenching into fists. "I loved you, Isla," he whispered to the empty room, the words barely audible through the silence that followed. "I loved you."

Across town, Isla woke up to a different kind of quiet.

The morning sunlight filtered through the curtains of Megan's guest room, casting a warm glow that softened the edges of the world. For the first time in what felt like forever, Isla felt a small sense of calm settle in her chest. She had barely moved all night, sleeping deeply despite the pain that throbbed in her bruised body.

She turned her head to find Megan sitting beside her, holding a steaming cup of coffee in her hands. The smile on her friend's face was a balm to Isla's weary soul.

"Morning, sleepyhead," Megan said, her voice gentle. She handed the coffee to Isla, who took it gratefully, inhaling the comforting aroma.

They sat in silence for a few moments, sipping their drinks and soaking in the peacefulness of the morning. Then, Megan broke the silence, a wistful smile on her face.

"Remember when we used to sneak out to the old treehouse behind my parents' place?" she said with a soft laugh. "We thought we were so rebellious, hiding out there with our snacks and flashlights."

Isla couldn't help but smile at the memory. "Yeah, we'd stay out there until your mom came looking for us. She always knew where we were, but she'd pretend to be so surprised when she found us."

Megan chuckled, her expression turning wistful. "I miss those days. Things were... simpler then."

A shadow passed over Megan's face, and Isla reached out to squeeze her hand. "I'm so sorry about your parents, Meg. I wish I'd been there for you more after the accident."

Megan's eyes softened, and she shook her head. "You had your own things going on, Isla. It's okay. That's why I took that job out of state—I needed a fresh start, a way to escape everything. But I'm glad I'm back, even if it's just for a little while."

She leaned in, pulling Isla into a gentle hug, careful not to press too hard against her bruises. "And I'm here for you now, okay? Whatever you need, we'll get through this together."

Isla blinked back the tears that welled in her eyes, grateful for Megan's unwavering support. "Thank you, Meg. I don't know what I'd do without you."

Megan smiled, but her expression grew serious as she glanced at the clock. "I need to run a few errands today, but I'll be back this afternoon. You should stay in and rest, okay? Call me if you need anything—anything at all."

Isla nodded, her heart squeezing with a mix of gratitude and fear. "I will. Be safe, okay?"

Megan gave her a reassuring squeeze before heading out, leaving Isla alone in the quiet house. For the first time, Isla allowed herself to hope that maybe, just maybe, she could find a way out of this nightmare.

Chapter Five:
The Scent Of Rain

Caleb slipped into his other persona—the charming mechanic who everyone in town knew and loved. At the body shop, he greeted his regulars with the same easy smile, masking the storm that raged within. He chatted with Mrs. Thompson, the elderly widow who trusted no one else with her vintage Buick, and laughed with Mr. Diaz, a local contractor whose truck always seemed to need a new part or two.

"Caleb, you're a lifesaver," Mrs. Thompson said as she paid for the repairs. "I don't know what I'd do without you."

Caleb flashed her a bright smile, tipping his cap. "Just doing my job, ma'am. You take care now."

As he handed over the keys, Mr. Diaz leaned in with a knowing grin. "So, when's the big day, huh? You and Isla tying the knot anytime soon?"

Caleb's smile faltered for a split second, but he quickly recovered. "We'll see," he said smoothly, the lie rolling off his tongue. "You know how it is, busy with work and all."

The praise from his customers soothed the edges of his bruised ego, but beneath the surface, a darker resolve took hold. When he finished his shift, he wasted no time heading toward Megan's place, his thoughts spiraling as he drove. He knew where they were— where Isla was hiding.

That evening, Caleb parked a few blocks away and slipped into the shadows near Megan's house. From the corner of the yard, he peered through the living room window, his breath catching when he saw Isla and Megan laughing together. The sound of Isla's joy, so light and unburdened, sent a wave of rage crashing through him. How could she smile like that, as if everything he'd done for her meant nothing?

He clenched his fists, taking a step closer, his mind buzzing with plans of retribution. But as he edged forward, his foot crunched against a piece of broken glass on the pavement. The sound shattered the stillness of the night, and he froze, his pulse hammering in his ears.

Inside, Isla and Megan turned toward the window, their expressions wary. Megan rose from the couch, peering through the glass window. "Did you hear that?" she whispered.

Isla nodded, her heart quickening with unease. "Yeah. Maybe it was just a stray cat or something."

Megan grabbed a flashlight and shined it outside, but the beam found nothing but empty space. "I don't see anything," she said, but her voice was tense, her grip on the flashlight tight.

They lingered at the window for another moment before Isla finally turned away, letting out a breath. "It's probably nothing," she muttered, trying to convince herself.

But as they settled back onto the couch, Caleb melted back into the shadows, retreating to his car with a twisted smile playing on his lips. He knew they hadn't seen him, but he had seen them. He knew where Isla was, and he knew she still feared him.

As he drove away, his mind churned with plans, dark and dangerous. And when the time came, he would make sure she understood the price of betraying him. As Caleb drove through the quiet streets, the hum of his car the only sound, his mind drifted back to a time long past—a time when life had been harder, when the weight of the world felt heavier on his shoulders.

He and Jace had grown up in foster homes, bouncing from one to another like unwanted pieces of furniture. Their parents had never been there for them, and it never took long for Caleb to sense that he and Jace were just... burdens. The endless parade of strangers who looked at them with pity or indifference only deepened the feeling that they were unwanted, cast off from a life they were never meant to have. In those years, Caleb learned to be protective. His younger brother, Jace, was all he had, and Caleb made it his mission to shield him from the pain of being left behind. He'd fought for his brother, and defended him in every new home they were thrown into, even when it meant facing down bullies twice his size. He didn't care. All that mattered was Jace. And for the most part, Jace looked up to him. Caleb was his hero, the one constant in a life that was anything but steady.

But that bond, that unshakable loyalty, didn't protect them from the world's harshness. As they got older, Jace started changing. The allure of the streets and the freedom they offered was too much for him. He fell in with the wrong crew. Caleb tried to stop him, tried to remind him of their bond, but Jace was no longer the kid who had idolized his older brother. He was a young man who sought power, respect, and escape from the things that had haunted them both.

The day Jace's world crashed down on him was the day Caleb's heart broke in a way it never had before. Jace had robbed an elderly woman—had beaten up her grandchildren in the process, just to get away. It wasn't the act itself that crushed Caleb; it was the fact that the police caught him. They took Jace away and sentenced him to years behind bars. Caleb had lost his brother once again, but this time, it was different.

This time, it wasn't some foster parent who sent Jace away. It wasn't some stranger who decided they didn't want them. It was Jace himself, lost in his choices. Caleb could feel the finality of it, the loneliness, the abandonment. For Caleb, it felt like his one true family, the only person who had ever really mattered, was being torn from him all over again.

He didn't know how to handle it. The rage that bubbled beneath the surface had nowhere to go, and it festered. It stayed with him, turning into an obsession. He had loved Jace. He had cared for him. And now, Jace was gone, a piece of his heart locked away in a prison cell. The bond they shared—the only family he had ever known—was broken.

And now, as he stared at the life he thought he could build with Isla, everything began to crumble again. Caleb couldn't help but see the parallels—how he'd given his all, how he'd done everything for her... and yet she was slipping away, just like Jace had. The anger simmered inside of him, hot and unforgiving. He knew this pain, this feeling of betrayal. He had lived through it once before. But this time, he would not let it go. Not without a fight.

Chapter Six:
Wrath Unleashed

T he morning light filtered through the curtains as Isla stirred on the couch, blinking against the sun that cast a warm glow over the living room. She sat up to find Megan bustling about, setting out plates on the small dining table. The smell of freshly brewed coffee filled the air, mingling with the scent of toast.

"Good morning, sunshine," Megan called out with a smile, glancing up from her preparations. "I made breakfast, but I have to run. One of my friends was supposed to meet me here, but she had a change of plans, so now I've got to meet her at this pub near downtown."

Isla frowned, feeling a pang of anxiety at the thought of being alone. "Are you sure you need to go? I'll be fine, but..."

Megan gave her a reassuring squeeze on the shoulder. "I won't be long, I promise. Besides, you could probably use a little time to yourself. I left the spare key in the kitchen drawer next to the stove, just in case you need to go out, but please be careful, okay?"

Isla managed a nod, trying to keep the unease from showing on her face. "Alright, I'll be careful. Thanks, Meg."

Megan gave her a quick hug, then grabbed her bag and rushed out the door, leaving Isla standing in the doorway, watching as her friend hurried to her car. A feeling of loneliness settled over her as she closed the door behind her.

She ate breakfast slowly, trying to savor the sense of normalcy, but the silence of the house soon became oppressive. She tried keeping herself busy—throwing a load of laundry into the washing machine, flipping through a magazine, and even picking up a book from Megan's shelf. But nothing held her attention for long.

Eventually, she found herself staring out the window, the walls of the house pressing in on her, making her feel trapped. She thought of the art studio, the one place where she felt truly free. Before she could talk herself out of it, she grabbed her bag, the spare key, and called for a taxi.

Outside, Caleb watched from the shadowed interior of his Mustang—a once-sleek '99 model now bearing the wear of years under his hands. The black paint was dulled by sun and dust, faint scratches tracing stories of past repairs. The scent of oil and old leather lingered in the cab, mixing with the quiet hum of the idling engine as he kept his eyes locked onto Isla's every move. When he saw her stepping out, locking the door behind her, and heading to the curb where the taxi would pick her up, his pulse quickened.

She had no idea. No idea how long he had been waiting for this, how many nights he had spent thinking about what he would do when he finally got his hands on her again. She thought she could run, thought she could escape him, but she was wrong.

Caleb's fingers flexed on the steering wheel as a slow, dark satisfaction unfurled in his chest. He had given her space, let her think she was safe. Now, it was time to remind her that she would never be free of him. He had molded her once before and shaped her to fit the world he had envisioned. And now, she would learn again—this time, without the illusions of choice.

He followed the taxi at a distance, careful to keep far enough behind to avoid being noticed. His grip on the steering wheel tightened as they drove across town, his mind racing with thoughts of what he would do next.

The taxi pulled up in front of the art studio, and Isla stepped out, casting a glance back over her shoulder before heading inside. Caleb parked his car a few blocks away, watching as she disappeared through the studio doors. A twisted satisfaction curled in his chest; she had no idea that he was right there, just a heartbeat away.

Isla stepped into the studio, breathing in the familiar scent of paint and canvas. The space was quiet and empty, just as she liked it. She immediately felt a sense of comfort wash over her as she began setting up her supplies, moving with a lightness in her step that she hadn't felt in weeks. As she gathered her brushes and squeezed paint onto her palette, she couldn't help but do a little twirl, letting herself feel the freedom of being back in her element.

She started painting, letting the strokes of her brush flow in a rhythm that matched the music playing softly from the studio's old radio. Her work took on a life of its own, vibrant colors swirling together to form an abstract expression of hope, breaking free from the chains that had held her.

Time slipped away, and by the time she finally stepped back from her easel, it was dark outside. She glanced at her phone and saw that it was nearly out of battery—only 3% left. She tried calling Megan, but the signal was poor, and the call dropped almost immediately. Isla frowned, trying again, but the result was the same. Frustrated, she gathered her things and headed outside, deciding to walk to a nearby gas station to use their phone or call another cab.

The air was cool against her skin as she stepped out onto the quiet street, the studio's lights fading behind her. She wrapped her coat tighter around herself, heading toward the neon glow of a distant gas station sign.

From the shadows, Caleb watched as Isla emerged, walking with her head down, focused on her phone. He moved quickly, slipping into his car and driving up the street, cutting the engine just as he approached her.

She didn't hear him until it was too late. The soft crunch of gravel underfoot made her glance up, but before she could react, Caleb was on her. His hand clamped over her mouth, and she struggled, trying to scream, but her voice was muffled against his palm. Her eyes went wide with terror as she recognized him, but he gave her no chance to fight back.

With a vicious shove, he forced her to the ground, knocking the breath from her lungs. He moved with the practiced ease of a man who had thought this through a hundred times, binding her wrists with rough rope and gagging her. Her eyes pleaded with him as he opened the trunk of his car, but Caleb's expression was cold, detached.

He hoisted her into the trunk with a grunt, slamming the lid shut before she could kick out or make any noise. He stood there for a moment, listening to her frantic, muffled cries from inside, the sound sending a shiver of satisfaction through him.

With one last glance around, he strode to the driver's side, yanking open the creaky door of his Mustang and sliding behind the wheel. He turned the key, the engine rumbling to life. He exhaled slowly, gripping the steering wheel tight as he pulled away from the curb, his headlights slicing through the darkness.

A few doors down, the fluorescent glow of a rundown gas station flickered against the pavement. The attendant inside, a lanky guy in a wrinkled uniform, yawned as he pushed open the door, a trash bag swinging at his side. He stepped onto the cracked pavement, rubbing his eyes against the night's chill. If he had come out just a minute sooner, he might have caught sight of the Mustang, of the way its tires left a faint screech against the asphalt as it disappeared into the night. But by the time he glanced up, there was nothing but an empty road and the distant hum of an engine fading into the dark.

Darkness. Tight space. The smell of rust and gasoline filling her lungs. Isla's breath came in ragged, panicked bursts as she lay crumpled in the trunk. *No, no, no—this isn't happening. Wake up. This has to be a nightmare.* Her heart pounded so violently it hurt. She twisted her wrists against the ropes, the fibers biting into her skin. *Think, Isla. Think. There has to be a way out.*

Tears blurred her vision, but she refused to break down. Not yet. She forced herself to take slow, shaky breaths. *Megan will realize I'm missing. Someone will look for me. They have to.*

Above, the muffled sound of Caleb humming sent a wave of nausea through her. He was enjoying this. The thought made her stomach turn. *I won't let him win. I won't be that girl again.*

Megan returned home that evening to an empty house. Her heart sank as she called out for Isla, but there was no reply. Panic began to claw at her chest as she hurried through the rooms, checking every corner and every door. She tried calling Isla's phone, but it went straight to voicemail.

She paced the living room, her mind racing. Isla wouldn't have left without telling her. Something was wrong—deeply wrong—and the fear settled like a heavy stone in her gut. Desperate for some kind of reassurance, Megan rushed to the kitchen, yanking open the drawer where she'd left the spare key. Her breath hitched. It was gone.

A wave of nausea rolled over her as she gripped the edge of the counter. If Isla had taken it, where had she gone? The walls of the house suddenly felt too close, suffocating. She reached for her phone again, her hands trembling, but she already knew. Isla wasn't answering. And Megan had no idea where to even start looking.

She sat there for a moment, trying to steady her breath, but the thoughts in her head raced faster than she could catch them. Isla is fine, she told herself, her mind repeating the mantra as if it could make it true. She'll walk in any second. She'll be okay.

But the uncertainty gnawed at her, refusing to let go. She needed something—anything—to calm her nerves. Her hand shook as she reached for the bottle of whiskey on the counter, unscrewing the cap and pouring herself a drink. The amber liquid sloshed into the glass, and she took the bottle and glass with her to the breakfast table, slumping into the chair as if it could anchor her to the present.

With a sigh, she lifted the glass to her lips, the burn of the alcohol doing little to ease the tight knot in her chest. She drank it down in one go, then poured herself another, the glass filling again with that same desperate hope that maybe, just maybe, the next sip would bring some peace. But all it did was make the room spin a little more.

Meanwhile, Caleb drove down a dark, winding road, his hands gripping the steering wheel. Isla lay in the trunk, every bump in the road jarring her battered body, tears streaming down her face as she struggled against the restraints. Fear and pain throbbed through her, but above all, she couldn't understand how this had happened—how he had found her, why he was doing this to her.

They reached the edge of a desolate field, far from the city lights, where the night seemed darker than anywhere else. Caleb dragged Isla from the trunk, ignoring her muffled cries and desperate attempts to fight back. He threw her to the ground, his breath coming in harsh, angry bursts.

"Please," Isla whimpered against the gag, her voice muffled but desperate. "Caleb, don't do this. You don't have to do this."

Caleb's jaw clenched. "You think you can just walk away from me, Isla? After everything?"

"I—" she tried to speak, but fear choked her words. "I never wanted this. Please, just let me go."

He only laughed, a hollow, bitter sound. "Too late for that."

With cold precision, he bound her legs, ignoring her as she struggled against the ropes, the desperation in her eyes cutting through the darkness. His heart pounded in his chest as he looked down at her, a twisted satisfaction mingling with the rage that still seethed beneath the surface.

"You think you can just leave me, Isla?" he snarled, his voice a harsh whisper that cut through the stillness of the night. He struck her, the blow landing with a sickening thud against her side. She gasped, pain exploding through her ribs, but she couldn't make a sound beyond the muffled cries against the gag.

He beat her again and again, each blow more savage than the last, until she lay gasping, struggling for breath, the stars spinning above her as the world faded in and out of focus. Blood trickled from a cut on her temple, her vision blurring with tears and pain.

Caleb's hands shook as he finally stepped back, staring down at her with a wild, crazed look in his eyes. He hadn't planned for this—not fully. He had wanted to hurt her, to make her pay for leaving him, but he hadn't thought about what would happen afterward.

But now, looking at her broken body, the realization crept in. He had gone too far. Panic clawed at him as he stared down at Isla, the life slowly fading from her eyes, the realization of what he had done crashing down on him like a wave.

He dragged her body deeper into the field, his breaths coming in panicked gasps. The earth was cold and unyielding beneath his hands as he dug, his mind numb with shock. He buried her quickly, roughly, covering her with dirt until only the dark, freshly turned earth marked the spot where she lay.

As he finished, he stepped back, staring at the grave he had made, his chest heaving. The reality of what he had done settled into the silence, and for the first time, Caleb felt the cold grip of fear tighten around his heart.

He stumbled back to his car, hands shaking, and drove away into the darkness, leaving behind the shattered remnants of the life he had destroyed.

Chapter Seven:
The Eye Approaches

Megan jolted awake, her body stiff and sore from the uncomfortable position she had fallen asleep in. Her head lay on the breakfast table, her phone clutched in her hand, the screen dark and unresponsive. She sat up, blinking against the harsh morning light that poured through the window. A surge of dread washed over her as she remembered the empty house and the unanswered calls from the night before.

"Isla?" Megan's voice cracked as she called out, even though she knew there would be no reply. The silence of the house pressed in around her, cold and heavy. Her heart pounded in her ears as she moved from room to room, checking each corner, each closet, hoping that maybe, just maybe, Isla had returned and was simply asleep, unaware of the frantic worry she'd caused. She checked the bedroom first, the sheets undisturbed.

Nothing. No trace of her.

A fresh wave of anxiety crashed over Megan, and she knew she couldn't stay in the house, not while every second felt like an eternity. She grabbed her keys and rushed out the door, her mind racing with questions. Where could Isla have gone? What if she was hurt somewhere, needing help?

Windows down. Air sharp against her skin. Megan sped through Barrowsville, eyes scanning every sidewalk, every doorway. She stopped at the local diner where Isla liked to grab coffee, then at the park where they used to go on long walks together. She even stopped at the small grocery store where Isla would sometimes pick up art supplies. She spoke with familiar faces—neighbors, friends, people who knew both her and Isla—but each time she asked if they had seen her, the answer was always the same.

"No, sorry, Megan. Haven't seen her."

Megan's chest tightened with each reply, her hope dwindling with every stop. She couldn't shake the feeling that something terrible had happened. And yet, she had to keep moving, had to keep searching.

Finally, she drove to the art studio, her hands gripping the steering wheel so tightly that her knuckles turned white. When she pulled into the parking lot, she saw Mrs. Harper, the studio's owner, just arriving, her car idling in the space closest to the door. Megan hurried out of her car and rushed over, catching Mrs. Harper just as she was about to step out of her vehicle.

"Mrs. Harper!" Megan's voice wavered as she called out, startling the older woman. Mrs. Harper turned, her brow furrowing with concern as she saw the desperation on Megan's face.

"Megan, dear, what's the matter?" she asked, stepping out of her car and closing the door behind her.

"It's Isla. She—she didn't come home last night, and I've been looking for her everywhere. Have you seen her? Did she come here yesterday or call you at all?" Megan's words tumbled out in a frantic rush.

Mrs. Harper's face softened, and she shook her head slowly. "No, I haven't seen her since last week. She was here painting like she always does, but I haven't heard from her since. Is she alright?"

Megan's voice caught in her throat, and she had to swallow the lump that rose up. "I don't know. I'm worried something's happened. This isn't like her."

Mrs. Harper reached out, placing a comforting hand on Megan's arm. "I'm sure she's okay, Megan. Isla's a strong woman, but... you're right. It's not like her to just disappear like this. If there's anything I can do, just let me know."

Megan's shoulders sagged with exhaustion and fear, and she bit her lip to hold back the tears that threatened to spill. "Thank you, Mrs. Harper. I just—if you hear anything, please, call me right away."

Mrs. Harper nodded, her expression serious. "Of course, dear. And you know, I've always thought the world of Isla. She's so talented, so full of promise. I've been thinking about gifting this studio to her once my loan is paid off, you know? I think she'd make something beautiful of it."

Megan forced a smile, but it felt hollow. "She'd love that. She's always felt at home here."

As Megan turned to leave, her heart heavy with worry, Mrs. Harper called out one last time. "I'll keep an eye out, Megan. We'll find her."

Megan managed a nod, but she felt defeated, the weight of Isla's absence pressing down on her like a physical ache. She drove back through town, scanning every corner, every face in the hopes that she might spot Isla, but it was like she had vanished into thin air.

Isla's sudden disappearance sent shockwaves through Barrowsville. For the first few days, the town whispered rumors—speculation and gossip spreading like wildfire. Some thought she had run off, maybe found a new lover, or decided to start fresh somewhere else. But those closest to her, especially Megan, knew that something was terribly wrong. Isla wasn't the kind of woman to vanish without a word or warning.

Megan's worry became desperation as she sat in the dimly lit police station, the fluorescent lights buzzing softly overhead. As she filled out the missing person report, each word felt like a weight pressing down on her chest. With every letter she wrote, a dreadful realization began to claw at her mind—*What if Caleb has her?*

Her hands shook slightly as she gripped the pen tighter, her thoughts racing. *What if he's hurt her?*

The thought sent a chill through her, making her movements clumsy and rushed. She hurriedly finished the paperwork, barely able to see straight through the fog of fear clouding her mind.

As she slid the report across the counter to the officer, her voice came out uneven and desperate, barely holding back the panic that had been rising within her all morning.

"I'm telling you, she wouldn't just leave,"

Megan insisted, looking up at the officer behind the desk, her eyes burning with unshed tears. "And she's afraid of her ex—Caleb. He's dangerous, he... he hurt her before."

The officer, a middle-aged man with thinning hair, gave her a sympathetic but skeptical look. "We'll file the report, ma'am, but you know adults are free to come and go as they please. A lot of the time, they turn up on their own."

He spoke with the kind of detachment that came from years of dealing with domestic disputes and runaway cases.

Megan's frustration boiled over, her desperation pushing her beyond the point of politeness. She leaned forward, gripping the edge of the desk as if she could anchor herself in the moment.

"She wouldn't leave without telling me. And Caleb—he's not right. He stalked her; he threatened her. She was going to file charges against him—we were supposed to come in together to get it filed, but we never made it. Please, you have to take this seriously."

Her voice cracked on the last word, echoing through the quiet station. Tears welled up in her eyes, spilling down her cheeks as she pleaded with the officer, hoping he would hear the truth in her voice, hoping he would understand that this was more than just a misunderstanding.

As the officer started to open his mouth to give another practiced response, a shadow fell over the counter. Detective Dexter Kane, who had been on his way out for lunch, paused as he overheard Megan's plea. He turned, his sharp gaze taking in the scene— Megan's tear-streaked face, the resignation in the officer's eyes, and the report lying on the counter between them.

"Hold up a second, Tom," Detective Kane said, his voice cutting through the air with authority. The officer, Tom, looked up in surprise as Kane took the report from his hands, glancing over the details quickly before focusing on Megan.

He studied her, noting the way her hands trembled and the raw edge of fear in her expression. "Ms. Jensen, is it?"

He asked, his voice firm yet gentle. Megan nodded, wiping her eyes with the back of her hand, trying to steady herself.

"Come with me," Detective Kane said, gesturing toward the hallway that led to his office. Megan followed him, her legs feeling unsteady as they walked past rows of desks and into a small room lined with shelves full of case files.

Kane closed the door behind them, motioning for her to sit down in the chair opposite his cluttered desk. He leaned against the edge, crossing his arms as he met her gaze head-on.

"Tell me everything you know about Caleb. Start from the beginning."

Megan took a shaky breath, trying to find the words through the haze of fear.

"Isla met Caleb a couple of years ago. He seemed nice at first, like he cared about her... but he changed. He became possessive and controlling. He would show up unannounced, go through her phone, accuse her of things that weren't true. And then... he started getting physical. Grabbing her arms too hard, throwing things when he was angry."

Kane's expression darkened as he listened, his jaw clenching subtly. He took a notepad from his desk and began jotting down details as Megan continued.

"She tried to leave him, but he wouldn't let her go. He started showing up at her job, following her around town. Isla was scared. We talked about filing a restraining order, and we were supposed to come here to do it, but then...," her voice broke, and she struggled to hold back another wave of tears.

"We never got the chance. Now she's gone, and I know he's involved. He has to be."

Detective Kane let out a slow breath, his eyes narrowing thoughtfully as he processed what Megan had told him.

"Ms. Jensen, I'm going to take this seriously," he said, his voice low and firm.

"I've seen cases like this before, where the system doesn't act fast enough, and people slip through the cracks. I won't let that happen here."

Megan met his gaze, hope flickering in her chest for the first time since Isla disappeared.

"Thank you, Detective. Please, just... find her. Find Isla before it's too late." Kane nodded, his expression resolute.

"I'll start by looking into Caleb's whereabouts. I'll need any contact information you have for him, places he might go, or anyone who might know him. I'll make sure the patrol officers know to keep an eye out for him, too."

As Megan provided him with the information she had, Kane's mind was already spinning with possibilities, with the threads of a case he knew would require patience and persistence to unravel. He couldn't shake the urgency in Megan's voice nor the fear that lingered in her eyes.

Meanwhile, across town, Caleb went about his day, his routine seemingly unbroken. At the body shop where he worked, he joked with the other mechanics and greeted customers with his usual charm, a mask that concealed the darker truth beneath.

A man came in, complaining about a rattle in his truck's engine. Caleb put on his friendly smile, the kind that came easily to him.

"No problem, I'll take a look under the hood for you. Might just be a loose bolt or something." He bent down to examine the engine, his face hidden from the customer's view, and his expression turned cold and calculating, the smile fading as quickly as it had appeared.

Later, a regular customer, an older woman, came in for a routine oil change.

"Caleb, I've been having some trouble with the brakes lately. Can you help me out?"

Caleb nodded, wiping his hands on a greasy rag.

"Sure thing, Ms. Johnson. I'll have it sorted out in no time."

As he worked, she mentioned Isla in passing.

"Say, I haven't seen Isla around lately. You two still an item?"

Caleb stiffened for a moment before forcing another easy smile.

"Nah, she's been busy with her art. Got her head buried in those paints, you know how she is."

Ms. Johnson chuckled, oblivious to the tension in his voice.

"That girl always did have a creative soul. Well, if you see her, tell her I said hi."

Caleb nodded, but as she turned away, his smile slipped, replaced by a tight-lipped frown. He watched her leave the shop, his mind racing with thoughts he tried to keep buried. He knew he had to maintain appearances.

As he closed up the shop that evening, Caleb's thoughts returned to Isla, to the last time he had seen her and the rush of power he'd felt. But for the first time, a sliver of doubt crept into his mind—*what if they found out? What if they figured out what he had done?*

He shook the thoughts away and climbed into his car, forcing himself to focus on the road ahead. But no matter how hard he tried, the darkness lingered, shadowing his every move as he drove deeper into the night.

As the moon dipped below the horizon, he drove by Megan's house again, his eyes scanning the windows for any sign of movement. But the house remained dark and quiet. Megan hadn't given up; he knew that much, but for now, she was in the dark.

He allowed himself a small, twisted smile as he drove away, his mind playing over the events of the past few days. He had won, for now. But somewhere deep down, a flicker of fear gnawed at him— a fear that his carefully constructed world was beginning to unravel, one thread at a time.

Chapter Eight:
A Cry In The Wind

Days turned into weeks, and still, there was no trace of Isla. Her absence left a void in Barrowsville, the kind that turned into murmured speculation and unease. Megan refused to let those whispers define the narrative. She became more vocal in her pleas for justice, her desperation spilling over into every conversation with the police.

"Do you even care that she's missing?" she demanded one morning, her voice rising as she spoke with Detective Kane outside the station. Her eyes were bloodshot, her hair disheveled from the sleepless nights spent scouring the town for any sign of Isla.

"She's out there somewhere, and you're just sitting around while time slips away!"

Detective Kane kept his expression calm, his gaze steady as he faced Megan.

"Ms. Jensen, I understand how you feel. I do. But we're following every lead, and these things take time. I promise you, I'm not letting this go cold."

Megan's shoulders slumped, and she buried her face in her hands for a moment before looking back up at him.

"You don't get it. I feel like every minute that passes is another minute she's slipping away, further into whatever nightmare she's trapped in."

Kane softened his tone, sensing the desperation in her voice.

"I hear you. I promise you, I won't stop looking until we find her. But I need you to trust me, alright?"

Megan nodded slowly, her hands still trembling as she tried to hold back the tears.

"I just... I need her back. She's my best friend."

Kane gave her a small, reassuring nod before turning toward his car. As he drove away, his mind turned over the next steps he had planned. He knew that finding Isla would mean getting to the heart of Caleb's secrets, and he intended to start peeling back those layers today.

That afternoon, Detective Kane pulled up in front of Caleb's body shop. The scent of motor oil and rubber filled the air, mixing with the distant hum of traffic. The sun beat down on the cracked pavement, casting long shadows across the row of cars lined up for repairs. Caleb was leaning against the open hood of a pickup truck, wiping his hands with a greasy rag, when he noticed Kane approaching. He straightened up, the easy smile he always wore slipping into place like a mask.

"Afternoon, Detective," Caleb called, his voice carefully casual.

"What brings you down to this part of town?" Kane mirrored the friendly tone, though his eyes never left Caleb's.

"Just checking in, thought I'd ask a few more questions. You know, since you were close to Isla."

Caleb's jaw tightened almost imperceptibly at the mention of Isla's name, but he quickly forced a chuckle.

"Yeah, well, I haven't seen her in weeks. Told the officers everything I knew already."

Kane leaned against a nearby car, folding his arms.

"I get that. But sometimes people remember things after they've had time to think. Maybe something you saw or heard around the time she went missing? Even the smallest detail could help."

Caleb rubbed the back of his neck, feigning thoughtfulness.

"Nah, can't say I do. Like I said, Isla and I weren't exactly talking much before she disappeared. She was always so... independent, you know?"

Kane raised an eyebrow, his expression remaining neutral.

"Funny, I heard she was staying close with a friend of hers after the split. Hardly sounds like she was eager to be on her own."

Caleb's face twitched at that, a flicker of irritation crossing his features before he quickly masked it with a smirk.

"Well, she always had a mind of her own. Maybe she wanted space from me, but that doesn't mean I know where she went."

Kane caught the slip, noting the way Caleb's smile didn't quite reach his eyes. He let the silence hang in the air for a moment, studying the tension in the other man's posture before speaking again.

"I get it. Breakups can be tough, especially when feelings are still raw. People don't always make the best decisions. But if you hear anything, give me a call, alright?"

He reached into his jacket pocket and pulled out a business card, extending it to Caleb.

"Come down to the station sometime this week. I'd like to get a little more background from you—just to help with the investigation. You might be able to point me in the right direction."

Caleb hesitated for a beat too long before taking the card. He managed a tight nod, his fingers gripping the edge of the card as if it might slip away.

"Sure, Detective. I'll do that."

Kane gave him a final once-over, noting the nervous glint in Caleb's eyes, before pushing off from the car.

"Thanks, Caleb. We appreciate your cooperation."

As Kane turned and walked back toward his car, he allowed a small, satisfied smile to curl the corner of his lips. He'd seen the momentary flash of panic in Caleb's eyes—the way the man's composure had cracked under the pressure.

He's hiding something, Kane thought, slipping into the driver's seat. But he knew better than to push too hard, too fast. He'd let Caleb sweat it out, let him feel the weight of the investigation bearing down on him.

Caleb stood in front of the shop, watching the detective's car pull away, his heart hammering in his chest. His mind raced with a thousand thoughts, each one darker than the last. He clenched the business card tightly in his hand, his knuckles turning white around the edges.

What if he figures it out? The thought gnawed at him, tearing through his carefully constructed sense of control. He felt the walls closing in, the noose tightening. He couldn't afford any mistakes, not now.

His frustration boiled over as he turned back toward the shop. He decided to close up early, his nerves fraying with every passing minute. As he hurried to lock the door, an elderly customer shuffled up the sidewalk, her expression puzzled as she saw the closed sign.

"Caleb, I thought you'd be open today. I've got an issue with my brakes—"

But before she could finish, Caleb brushed past her, his shoulder bumping into her with enough force to send her stumbling backward. She nearly lost her balance, catching herself on a nearby car.

"Watch where you're going, lady!"

Caleb snapped, his voice harsh and uncharacteristically venomous. The woman's eyes widened in shock, and a few passersby on the sidewalk turned to watch the scene unfold, their murmured whispers cutting through the air.

"Hey, no need to be rude," a man called out from the crowd, his brow furrowed as he stepped forward. Others nodded in agreement, their curious stares making Caleb's skin itch with irritation.

Caleb shot them all a glare, his face flushed with anger, before hurrying to his car. He felt their eyes on him as he fumbled with his keys, the pressure of their judgment tightening around his chest. He climbed into his car and sped off, leaving behind the whispers and curious glances that followed him down the street.

From across the road, Detective Kane sat in his unmarked car, watching the entire scene unfold through his windshield. He took in the way Caleb's demeanor had shifted, the barely restrained anger that had bubbled to the surface when he thought no one was looking.

Kane's expression remained unreadable as he noted Caleb's erratic behavior, but a cold certainty settled in his gut.

He's losing control, Kane thought, a grim determination settling over him. He knew now that Caleb was involved, and he intended to find out just how deep those secrets ran.

Chapter Nine:
The Second Surge

Caleb's mind was a whirlwind as he pulled into the gas station, his pulse hammering in his throat. His hands trembled as he reached for the half-empty bottle of water sitting in the cup holder, desperate for something to steady himself. He twisted off the cap and took a deep gulp—only to gag as the warm, stale liquid hit his tongue. Cursing, he spat it out onto the pavement, wiping his mouth with the back of his hand. His nerves were shot, his thoughts spiraling. The conversation with Detective Kane played over and over in his mind, each word digging deeper into his panic.

He parked at a pump, stepped out, and hurriedly started the flow of gas. He kept glancing around, his gaze darting from one face to another—each stranger passing by seemed to linger on him a second too long. He imagined their whispers, their eyes peering through his carefully constructed facade. His pulse pounded in his ears, drowning out the hum of the station.

He didn't realize he had been staring into space until the acrid smell of gasoline hit his nostrils. Caleb snapped back to reality, noticing the gas was spilling over the edge of his tank, soaking into his shoes and splashing onto his clothes. He cursed under his breath, hurriedly yanking the nozzle out and fumbling to hang it back on the pump. The pungent scent of fuel clung to him, and he wiped his hands on his jeans, only spreading the slick, oily residue further.

"Dammit," he muttered, barely able to contain the tremor in his voice as he climbed back into his car. The gasoline seeped into the fabric of his seat, filling the cab with a sharp, nauseating odor. He needed to get home—needed to wash off the stench and calm his racing mind.

When he finally stumbled through the front door of his small, dingy house, Caleb's anxiety had twisted into a full-blown frenzy. The once neat space had turned chaotic over the past few weeks— discarded food containers cluttered the countertops, clothes lay in heaps on the floor, and dust gathered in the corners. He barely noticed the mess anymore; all he could think about was the gasoline clinging to his skin.

He stripped off his clothes and stepped into the shower, turning the water on full blast. As the scalding water pounded against his back, Caleb scrubbed at his arms and chest as if he could wash away more than just the smell—wash away the guilt, the fear, the memory of Isla's terrified eyes. But the panic still thudded in his chest, unrelenting, and soon he found himself punching the shower walls, each strike sending a dull ache through his knuckles.

"Get a grip, get a grip," he muttered to himself between ragged breaths. He stepped out of the shower, dripping wet, and wrapped a towel around his waist. But as he moved into the bedroom, a loud, frantic banging at the door froze him in place.

Caleb's heart jumped into his throat, and for a moment, he was sure it was the police. His mind flashed with images of being handcuffed, of Detective Kane's accusing eyes. He crept to the hallway, peering out of the front door's peephole, only to see Megan's familiar face twisted in anger as she pounded her fist against the door.

"Caleb! I know you're in there!" she shouted, her voice sharp enough to cut through the air. "Open the door, damn it! Did you do something to Isla?"

Caleb's breath hitched, and he backed away from the door as if it might suddenly fly open. He could hear her demanding to check the house, her words muffled but filled with desperation. He clamped a hand over his mouth, trying to silence his own heavy breathing as she continued to bang against the wood.

"Please, just open the door, Caleb! I need to know the truth!"

Megan's voice wavered, and for a moment, Caleb thought she might break down right there on his porch. But then, just as suddenly as she had arrived, the banging stopped.

Caleb listened to the sound of her footsteps retreating, followed by the rumble of her car engine. He rushed to the window, parting the curtains just enough to see Megan drive away, her taillights disappearing into the darkness.

He sank to the floor, gripping his hair in both hands, pulling until his scalp burned. His chest heaved, and he felt the walls of his house pressing in on him, suffocating him with their narrow confines. He couldn't stay here—he needed to escape, even if just for a few hours.

Caleb found himself at the local pub, the lights dim, the air thick with the scent of stale beer. He took one shot, then another, desperate for the burn to drown out the roaring storm in his head. But no matter how many glasses he emptied, he couldn't shake the image of Isla's face or the sound of Megan's accusing voice.

"Hey, that's enough for you, buddy," the bartender said, her voice firm as she pulled the bottle out of his reach. She was a no-nonsense woman in her fifties, with a stern expression that brooked no argument.

Caleb's frustration boiled over, and he slammed his empty glass on the counter.

"You don't get to tell me when I've had enough!" he snapped, his words slurring together.

"Just do your damn job and pour me another."

The bartender crossed her arms, unimpressed.

"You're done, Caleb. I'm not serving you anymore. Now get out of my bar before I call the cops."

Caleb's eyes flashed with anger, and he hurled a string of insults at her, his voice rising above the hum of conversation. But she stood her ground, and the other patrons began to turn in their seats, staring at the scene he was causing. Caleb could feel their judgment like a weight on his chest, pressing down until he could barely breathe.

Finally, he stumbled out of the bar, his head swimming as he fumbled for his car keys. He leaned against the door of his vehicle, sucking in the cool night air as if it could cleanse the chaos raging inside him. His hands shook as he fumbled with the keys, and then, without warning, the floodgates opened.

He slid into the driver's seat and broke down, the sobs wracking his body with a force that left him breathless.

"I'm sorry, Isla," he choked out, his voice cracking as he clung to the steering wheel.

"Forgive me. I hurt you. You didn't deserve it. I didn't deserve you..."

For a moment, it seemed like the remorse might consume him. But then, like a shadow creeping back into the light, his pride slithered back into place. He wiped the tears from his face, his expression hardening as he muttered under his breath, convincing himself of the lie he'd repeated so many times before.

"She had it coming. If she'd just listened... if she'd just stayed where she belonged..."

Across the lot, Detective Kane watched the scene from the shadowed interior of his unmarked car. He'd seen Caleb's outburst in the bar, his breakdown in the car, and the moment when his face twisted back into that familiar mask of anger. Kane's fingers drummed against the steering wheel as he waited for Caleb to make his next move.

When Caleb finally started the engine and pulled out of the lot, Kane followed at a safe distance, his headlights off.

Caleb drove his car back to the fields on the edge of town, where the storm had once hidden the evidence of his crime. Kane's jaw clenched as he kept his focus on Caleb's taillights, his mind working through the steps of what he'd need to do next.

The night air was thick and humid as Caleb's car rolled to a stop in the middle of the field. He left the engine running, the beams casting long shadows over the soaked earth. The ground was still damp from the last heavy rain, the mud pulling at his boots as he staggered to the spot he remembered all too well.

He began to dig frantically, first with the shovel, then with his bare hands, shoveling the wet earth aside in desperate haste.

"Gotta move her, gotta hide it better," he muttered, his breath coming in short, desperate gasps. He didn't hear the approach of footsteps over the squelching mud until it was too late.

A flashlight beam cut through the darkness, illuminating Caleb in his frantic digging. He froze, spinning around to face the blinding lights of a car parked behind his own.

Detective Kane stepped out; his gun trained steadily on Caleb.

"Don't move, Caleb," he ordered, his voice carrying through the still night.

Caleb's hands trembled, his mind racing for an escape, but all he could see was the unyielding stare of the detective and the damning light that exposed everything he'd tried to bury.

Chapter Ten:
Thunder's Final Roar

L ightning tore through the night sky, illuminating the grim scene for a brief second, followed by a crack of thunder that seemed to shake the very ground beneath them.

Caleb stared at Detective Kane through the downpour, blinking against the water streaming down his face.

"Put down the shovel, Caleb!"

Kane's voice boomed over the sound of the rain, his stance unwavering, his gun still aimed at Caleb.

"Turn around and get on your knees. Now!"

The rain came down harder, soaking both men to the bone, but neither moved. Caleb's eyes darted between the detective and the heavens, his face twisted in a mixture of fear, defiance, and something else—something almost like desperation. His chest rose and fell with ragged breaths as he stared up at the dark, swirling sky—searching for a divine intervention that would never come. "You don't understand!"

Caleb shouted, his voice breaking, barely audible over the pounding rain.

"Have you ever loved anyone, Detective? Really loved them?"

His words came out in a manic rush, frantic and slurred from the alcohol still buzzing in his veins.

"I loved Isla! I loved her more than anything, but she... she kept trying to leave! She wouldn't stay! It was an accident, I didn't mean for it to happen, you have to believe me!"

Kane's expression hardened, his jaw set in a tight line. He'd heard these stories before—men who tried to twist their violence into something noble, tried to make their control sound like devotion. But he wasn't about to be swayed by Caleb's frantic pleas.

Slowly, Kane let his car door fall shut behind him with a muted thud. Rain slicked his hair to his forehead, his coat growing heavy with water, but he didn't waver. His boots sank into the mud with each step, the wet ground sucking at his soles as he moved forward, his steps steady, calculated.

Caleb's chest rose and fell in ragged gasps, his wide eyes darting between Kane and the gun in his own trembling hand. He took a step back, shaking his head, mumbling something under his breath—maybe another excuse, maybe a plea. But Kane didn't stop. He advanced slowly, each step deliberate, closing the space between them just enough to make Caleb feel the walls pressing in.

"Stop lying to yourself, Caleb," Kane called out, his voice cutting through the rain like a blade.

"This isn't love—it's control. Manipulation. You took her freedom, her safety... her life. You don't get to rewrite what you did."

Kane stopped a few feet away, just outside Caleb's reach, his stance firm but cautious. Caleb's face contorted with rage, the last thread of his composure snapping as Kane's words cut through the fog of alcohol and self-pity. His grip on the shovel tightened, his body trembling with barely contained fury.

"You don't know anything about me!" he shouted, stepping forward.

"You're just a cop—married to your damn job! You've never loved anyone! You don't know what it's like to feel everything slipping away—how far you'd go to keep it!"

Kane's eyes never wavered, even as Caleb took another step closer, the shovel still clenched in his fists. "What you feel isn't love, Caleb. It's fear—fear of losing control. But you lost it the moment you laid a hand on her."

Caleb's face twisted, his breath coming in ragged gasps. He took another step toward Kane, closing the distance between them inch by inch, the rain soaking through his clothes and turning the ground beneath his boots to sludge. He could barely feel the cold—could barely think past the roaring in his ears.

Kane steadied his aim, raising his voice above the storm.

"Don't make me do this, Caleb. Drop the shovel and get on your knees!"

But Caleb's mind was too far gone, spiraling deeper into the darkness that had consumed him. He could feel his control slipping like mud through his fingers, and Kane's unwavering gaze only made the panic coil tighter in his gut. He let out a guttural scream, his muscles tensing as he lunged toward the detective, raising the shovel like a weapon.

Two shots cracked through the night, slicing through the thunder and rain. The shovel flew from Caleb's grip, spinning into the mud, as his body jolted with the impact. He stumbled forward, the weight of the bullets driving him to his knees. His hand clutched at his side, blood mingling with the rainwater that poured down his face and soaked the earth beneath him.

Detective Kane staggered back, his ears ringing from the gunfire, barely able to keep his balance as the adrenaline pulsed through him. He pressed a hand to his forehead, feeling the shallow cut where the edge of the shovel had grazed his temple, but he kept his focus on Caleb. His breaths came in harsh, uneven gasps, but he held his ground, refusing to let his guard drop until it was over.

Caleb collapsed into the mud, his gasps turning wet and gurgling as he fought for breath. The rain pelted down on him, each drop a drumbeat in the chaotic rhythm of the night. He tried to speak, his lips moving silently, but the strength was draining from his body, the darkness closing in around the edges of his vision.

More squad cars arrived, their lights cutting through the storm, red and blue flashing against the backdrop of rain-soaked fields. Officers rushed forward, their shouts muffled by the downpour, but Kane held up a hand to keep them back. He kept his eyes on Caleb, watching as the fight drained out of him, as the life seeped away.

Caleb's body went limp in the mud, his breath rattling out one last time as the rain continued to fall. He lay just a few feet from the spot where he had buried Isla, the place where his carefully constructed lies had finally come undone. The ground that had once hidden his crime now bore witness to his end.

Kane lowered his gun, letting out a long, shaky breath as he holstered the weapon. He looked down at Caleb's lifeless form, feeling the weight of the night settle heavily on his shoulders. He knew the case wasn't over—not with the evidence still to be filed, the reports to be written, and the trial still ahead if justice was to be served for Isla. But on that rain-soaked field, justice had come, raw and unceremonious, in the only way it could.

As the other officers moved in to secure the scene, Detective Kane turned his face up to the sky, letting the rain wash over him. He could still feel the throb of his pulse in his head, the echo of Caleb's desperate words, but he pushed it aside, focusing instead on the quiet resolve that kept him standing.

The night would pass, the storm would move on, but the truth would remain—etched into the earth, like a scar that could never fully heal.

Chapter Eleven:
Stillness From The Ruins

The following morning, Barrowsville woke to a story that would shake the town to its core. The news flashed across television screens and mobile phones: *Local Business Owner Caleb Whitfield Found Dead in Standoff with Police; Missing Woman's Body Recovered.*

Shock rippled through the town. The man they thought they knew—a helpful neighbor, a skilled mechanic, the one who always wore a polite smile and offered a kind word—had been unmasked as a monster. It seemed impossible to some, but as the details emerged, the shock deepened. His business clients, friends, and even the patrons at his favorite diner couldn't reconcile the charming face they'd known with the reality of his actions.

Old rumors resurfaced—stories of Caleb's temper, hushed whispers from women who had worked at the body shop but left abruptly, never mentioning why. A few brave souls came forward, revealing past encounters that painted a darker, more sinister portrait of the man who had once blended so seamlessly into their lives. The town realized that Caleb's smooth exterior had hidden the truth for far too long.

Isla's story spread beyond the borders of Barrowsville, becoming a symbol of resilience and a call to action. Women from neighboring towns shared their own stories of fear and survival, emboldened by Isla's memory and the message that even the darkest secrets could not remain hidden forever.

In the midst of the town's upheaval, Megan stood at the center of it all, her heart heavy with grief but burning with a new sense of purpose. She took to the small town's community center, where she had organized a gathering for survivors of domestic violence. Her voice shook as she spoke, but there was a fire behind her eyes. "Isla was my best friend," she began, her voice carrying through the room. "She was strong and kind, and she deserved more than what happened to her. And if we can help even one woman find her way out before it's too late, then we'll have done right by her."

The support group grew rapidly, drawing women from all over, some with stories as tragic as Isla's and others who had managed to escape just in time. Megan found healing in helping them, in turning her friend's death into a force for change. The ache of loss would never fully leave her, but it transformed into a fierce determination to make sure no one else had to suffer in silence.

One evening, after a particularly difficult meeting, Megan found herself standing outside the community center, lost in her thoughts. The air was cool, the sun dipping low on the horizon, when Detective Kane approached her, his hands tucked into his coat pockets.

"Megan," he said, his voice gentler than she'd ever heard it. "How are you holding up?"

Megan offered a small, tired smile.

"Some days are better than others," she admitted. "But I think... I think Isla would be proud of what we're trying to do here."

Kane nodded, the corner of his mouth twitching into the hint of a smile.

"She would be. You've turned this into something meaningful. A lot of people wouldn't have the strength to do that."

They stood in silence for a moment, both gazing out at the quiet town. Then, Megan turned to face him, her expression more serious.

"Thank you, Detective. For believing me when no one else would. For bringing Isla back to us, even if it wasn't the way I'd hoped."

Kane looked down, a shadow passing over his features.

"I just wish... I wish I could have gotten to her sooner," he said, his voice rough.

"You were right about Caleb all along. And you never stopped fighting for her."

Megan placed a hand on his arm, her grip firm.

"And you saw through his lies when others wouldn't. That counts for something, Kane."

He glanced over at her, a hint of appreciation in his eyes, but it was clear that the events of that night still lingered in his mind. As he had stood in that rain-soaked field, gun in hand and Caleb bleeding out before him, he'd felt a hollowness settle in his chest—a sense that justice, though served, had come too late.

Chapter Twelve:
From The Ashes

In the days that followed, the local media praised Detective Kane for his dedication to solving the case. The town's mayor presented him with a plaque at a small ceremony, thanking him for his service and bravery. Kane accepted it with a polite nod, but he could barely muster a smile for the cameras. The recognition didn't sit right with him; it felt too much like celebrating a victory in a battle that should never have been fought.

After the ceremony, as he slipped away from the crowd, he found Megan waiting outside, leaning against the hood of her car. She watched him with a knowing look, seeing through the polite mask he wore for the public.

"You're not much for accolades, are you?" she asked, a faint smirk on her lips.

Kane shrugged, exhaling slowly. "Not when the real work's just beginning. There's a lot of people out there like Caleb. A lot of women who need someone to listen when they're scared." He met her gaze, and for a moment, there was a flicker of hope behind the weariness in his eyes.

Megan nodded, her own eyes misting with unshed tears. "Maybe we'll both find some peace in that," she said softly. "In knowing that Isla's story won't be forgotten."

Kane offered her a small, genuine smile, one that reached his eyes for the first time since the night in the field. "I think she'd be proud of you too, Megan."

"Thank you," Megan whispered, her voice soft but steady. "For everything you've done. I... I didn't expect this kind of kindness. After everything."

Kane took a step closer, his voice low, sincere. "Sometimes, we don't realize how much we need someone until they show up when it matters most." He paused, his gaze softening as it met hers. "I know I didn't expect to find someone like you in all this, either."

Megan hesitated for a moment, a flicker of uncertainty crossing her face. But something in Kane's gaze steadied her, an unspoken promise that they weren't alone in this.

"Do you think..." Megan began, her voice barely above a whisper, "that we could actually get past all of this?"

Kane's expression softened, and for the first time in what felt like forever, he allowed himself to hope.

"I don't know," he said quietly, his voice rough—but honest.

"But I think we could try. We've been through hell, but maybe that means we've learned something along the way. Something that could get us through."

Megan let out a breath, her chest tightening with emotion. She had never imagined that she would find someone in the aftermath of everything, someone who understood the weight of her grief, the way the world had been forever changed. And yet, here Kane was— steadfast, present, willing to face whatever came next with her.

"I think I'd like that," she said, her voice barely above a whisper.

"I think I'd like to try."

Kane stepped closer, gently placing his hand on her shoulder, his touch grounding her.

"Then we'll figure it out," he said softly, offering a small but genuine smile.

"One step at a time."

At that moment, everything seemed to slow—her heart, her thoughts, the world around them. Megan found herself clinging to the hope Kane had offered, a fragile thread of connection woven through the ashes of their pasts.

As they stood together, the weight of everything they had faced still lingered, but there was something else now, too—an undeniable bond. It wasn't perfect, it wasn't neat, but it was real. And for the first time in what felt like forever, Megan wasn't alone.

They stood there in the twilight, hand in hand, two people bound by loss but finding a path forward in the wake of tragedy.

As Megan and Kane stood in the fading light, the world seemed to settle around them, quiet and heavy. But in the distance, in the shadows of their new beginning, another figure lurked—one who had spent years in his own prison, consumed by thoughts of a different kind of loss.

Jace had just gotten out of prison a few days ago. Eight years behind bars for theft and aggravated battery, but those years had been nothing compared to the eternity he'd spent thinking about his brother. Caleb. His flesh and blood. The only person who had ever had his back. And now he was gone.

He sat in the driver's seat of his beat-up, rusted pickup truck, parked a few hundred yards from the edge of the street. The truck, a faded green Chevy, was an old model that had seen better days. He gripped the steering wheel tightly, his knuckles white in the dim light of the early evening. The crumpled newspaper in his lap crinkled as Jace picked it up, the headline glaring at him: *Kane Solves Tragic Murder, Brings Justice to Local Town*. The bold letters mocked him, daring him to read on. Beneath it, a photo of Detective Kane stood stoically in front of a police car, his face set in that trademark expression of calm determination. Jace's fingers clenched around the paper as his eyes moved down the page.

A few paragraphs down was Megan's picture, framed by the words, *Best Friend Speaks Out on Loss.* The text beneath it dripped with praise for the "Brave Young Woman" who had endured so much, offering a glimpse into her grief. But it didn't take much for Jace to notice the nasty things Megan had said about Caleb—her words twisted to fit her story of loss and grief. As Jace read, he could almost hear her voice, filled with righteous indignation.

Jace's eyes narrowed, a slow sneer curling on his lips.

"Gotcha..." he muttered to himself, the words dripping with venom.

There they were, less than 50 yards away—Kane, standing there with that smug, self-righteous air, his arms wrapped around Megan as if he'd done nothing wrong.

Jace's jaw clenched, a low growl rumbling in his throat. His grip on the wheel tightened even more, the silence in the truck thickening, suffocating him. His eyes flicked between the gun on the passenger seat and the photo of Kane. A cold chill swept over him.

His breath quickened, chest tightening. His mind was racing, planning, calculating the next move—the one that had burned a hole in him since the moment he'd set foot back in this town.

They think it's over. They have no idea what I'm capable of.

The gun felt heavier in his hands as he reached for it, his fingers itching to feel its cold weight. He didn't care about justice. He didn't care about redemption. This was about one thing and one thing only—revenge.

Kane had killed Caleb. And Jace wasn't going to let that slide. Not now, not ever.

The truck rumbled to life as Jace shoved it into gear, the engine groaning under the weight of his fury. His eyes locked on the figures ahead, and he drove forward, a man on a mission. The air inside the truck grew thicker with every mile, his pulse pounding in his ears.

Tonight, it wasn't about right or wrong. It wasn't about the law.

Tonight, it was about Caleb.

And Jace wasn't leaving town until a debt was paid in blood.

To Be Continued...

A Note to My Readers

Dear Readers,

Thank you for choosing to embark on the emotional journey of *I Didn't Deserve You*. Caleb and Isla's story is one of pain, redemption, and the search for healing—a reflection of the struggles that many of us face in life. Your willingness to walk alongside them as they navigate their trials means more to me than words can express.

Writing this book was a deeply personal and heartfelt process. It's my hope that their story resonated with you—whether it stirred emotions, offered a sense of understanding, or reminded you of the strength we all carry within.

Your support as a reader brings stories like this to life. Thank you for keeping this journey in your heart and stay tuned for Book 2.

With deepest gratitude,

More from August Clay

If *I Didn't Deserve You* spoke to your heart, I invite you to explore another story close to mine—***The House on Maplewood Lane: The Past Returns Home.***

This emotional suspense novel uncovers the quiet devastation of generational trauma, the weight of silence, and the haunting truths that often live within the walls we call home. It's a gripping and tender narrative that dives into the human spirit's resilience— perfect for readers who value heart, mystery, and healing.

The House on Maplewood Lane is available now on all digital platforms.

To stay connected, share your thoughts, or be the first to know about upcoming releases, you can follow me on social media or visit my website.

🌐 **www.augustclaystories.com**

📷 Instagram: @ac_short_stories

Let's keep the conversation going.

Stories connect us and I'd love to hear how these pages touched yours.

www.ingramcontent.com/pod-product-compliance
Lightning Source LLC
Chambersburg PA
CBHW051328120626
46547CB00015B/2452